What You Want

Joan Johnston

First published 1998 by:
Diamond Twig
5 Bentinck Road
Newcastle upon Tyne
NE4 6UT
Tel/Fax: (0191) 273 5326
Email: poetics@nildram.co.uk

Typeset in Palatino 10pt

Printed by Peterson Printers, South Shields

© Joan Johnston 1998

ISBN 0 9520090 3 X

Diamond Twig acknowledges the
financial assistance of Northern Arts

and The Echo Room Press, Editor Brendan Cleary

for Mam
1922 – 1997

Acknowledgements

Acknowledgements are due to the editors of the following publications in which some of these poems first appeared:
The Rialto, Fatchance, The Wide Skirt, Smith's Knoll, Writing Women.
Also from the Pamphlet 'Breathing In' published by Flarestack 1997.

Thanks are due to The Arvon Foundation and Northern Arts for writer's bursaries awarded in 1995 and 1998.

I would also like to thank Gillian Allnutt and Margaret Wilkinson for their extraordinary 'Inside Out' writing workshops and Brendan Cleary for his generosity and good counsel.

Above all, my thanks to Mark, Ben and Jamie. Without the space they give me these poems may never have appeared.

Contents

- 9 The cupboard
- 10 Burial
- 11 Maybe this'll be the day
- 12 Looking for grandma
- 13 Kitchen
- 14 Making it
- 15 Where she lived
- 16 No-one
- 17 Safe
- 18 On getting the pink linen dress
- 19 Petticoats
- 20 Cleanliness
- 21 Carried away
- 22 Ian's dad
- 23 Divorce 1945
- 24 Inside mother's wardrobe
- 25 Marksmen
- 26 Brenda
- 27 Aftermath
- 28 Abstract painting
- 29 Beached
- 30 Losing it
- 30 The stone pickers
- 32 Come close
- 33 You
- 34 Apart
- 35 D.I.Y.

36 My first winter like this
37 Caravan
38 What you want

When I was about 12 I wrote my first poem after watching a television documentary about prisoners on Death Row. That programme scared me, but not as much as the thought of someone reading my poem. I never told anyone I'd written it. No-one's ever seen it.

Poetry was always something other people did. People I didn't know. People who didn't live in the north of England. People whose parents didn't read The Woman's Own or The Football Pink or How I Play Snooker by Fred Davis. When I was 13 my Nanna died. Secretly I tried to write about her. I thought I ought to call her my Grandmother. I didn't know it was OK to write about the way she used to spit into the back of the fire and make it sizzle. Or how I'd miss her smell. You couldn't put that in a poem.

I tried hard to be A Writer but I never seemed to have the right kind of Experiences. Ian's Dad, the kitchen cupboard, the miracle of Teeda Hair Straightening Cream were not enough, were not the stuff of Great Poems. So I went down the Bigg Market with the girls instead and the writing stopped. No-one had to know I'd even tried it. It was a relief to be normal.

When my first son was born in 1985 I found a writing group that had a creche. I often say I would have joined any course at that time if it had a creche:

Arabic, Ancient Egyptian Mummification, Stick Dressing. But I'm not so sure. I think I knew what I was doing, what I wanted.

That was when I began again. We are very lucky to have so many good writers in this region who are also good tutors, good guides. When I look back through all the old notebooks that I filled at so many early writing workshops two things happen: my toes curl up with embarrassment a lot and I remember how none of these people were ever dismissive of my work. I remember careful listening, tact and encouragement.

The story of everyone's life is a story of the past, and my poems in this book were written then. I made them all up out of what I had. Reading them over I can remember where I was when each one was started, what I thought each one was going to be about. To me they are all different from each other. I seem to hear a lot of voices - but it's still a relief to be normal.

The cupboard

I meet her in a dream cafe
where we eat ice-cream
and I admire the embroidery
on her yellow dress.
And the next day, missing her,
in order to feel how she's real and dead
I look in the cupboard.
You can always find your dead mother
in her kitchen cupboard -
Crown Royal
Carlton Ware
Porcelain
Apostle Spoons
My Very Own Plate.

Burial

It's a summer funeral
but I know already
that when the snowdrops come up
in the old kettle by your door
I'll want to push them back.

Maybe this'll be the day

when the boat comes up Bottle Bank,
when I'll glance up from the sink
to see the Swing Bridge opening,
the pigeons all turning into pigs that fly.
Maybe today's the day when that big boat
will just float over the cobbles
and dock at the end of Saltwell Road,
spilling into my lap its cargo of
work for the men
a new leg for Bob
shoes for the bairns
a whole crateful of inside toilets
best butter from the country
fresh elbow grease
and bonny little bottles of Evening in Paris.

Looking for grandma

Because of all the laced-up shoes
I know their men are in France
and because of all their hats
I know the women are dead now,
their children old.
I find her at the front
facing the camera, holding the baby.
And because of the sepia embroidery
on the fine woollen shawl
I know there was blue then
and yellow and green.

Kitchen

It's rained all day.
Windows dribble,
the house steams.
In the kitchen in a large hat
Great-grandma's suddenly stirring
and marvelling at the ease
of the washing machine.
I breathe in, wash up,
noticing sideways her hat pin
which I've got in the silver box
upstairs.

Making it

I've modelled it on the old Bergere
replacing the chip straw and pipe clay
with this rabbit fur scrounged from Davidson's.
The lining's just a piece of scrim,
an oddment from the factory. It's all cadged.
Scraps. My little bit of frippery.
I'm hanging on for the right silk ribbon
in a colour to set it off nice.
There's a war on pet, we're scrimping
but it doesn't mean we can't have pink.

Where she lived

Grove.
Road.
Avenue.
Gardens.
In her last house,
empty now.
Close.

No-one

I get the idea it can climb stairs
so I place it at the bottom
and watch it through the bannisters.

I get the idea that it can swim
so I fill the tub and tempt it in
by whispering.

I get the idea it likes music
so I breathe in and hum to it,
pausing between the verses.

I get the idea that no-one's coming
so I leave it clutching air.
By the time I count to a hundred

they'll be here.

Safe

Gran had a way with fires,
made coaxing an art
and taught me how kindling
is also a cradle of a word.
One night she let me light it,
using a spill from the brass galleon
and she did old magic,
threw sugar on it.

Later, tucked in, I heard her
setting the table for breakfast,
the trains in the distance.

On getting the pink linen dress

Something fancy, perhaps in red
said mother. And maybe in a larger size
just to be on the safe side ?
This one suits you. That one's nice.
She lied.
A little shorter, a neat white collar,
but not in linen she insisted.

Some people get new ones every year
I whispered.

Petticoats

Frilled edges. It's a pity
not to let them show.
Just an inch of white
below the grey.
I have three brothers
so I wear petticoats a lot.
Your slip's showing, they sometimes say.
It's not a slip. When I have
a daughter she will be
as pretty as a picture
and we will wear each other's.

Cleanliness

Cleanliness is a night gown
on Sunday night. Sprigged
and starched to the scrubbed neck
and watching Dr Finlay's Casebook.
'Janet is a nice name' my mother says,
pressing the sheets stiff
with a steaming iron.

The bed is straight and tight,
smells of fresh air.
Outside over the wall
an owl hoots in the quiet rain.
On Sundays when I grow up
my bed will loosen
and billow and I will choose
soft skin for sleep.

Carried away

Everyone says it's dangerous
at the bottom of Loffler's Field:

Eva has a scar on her knee
like a long exclamation mark

and she's got me. With my head against
her shoulder, my feet on her feet

we goose-step together under
the coat. Far off Dad's shouting.

He thinks I'm lost. I'm not.

Ian's dad

I think I can do it
but I can't. I spill it
on the carpet and Ian's dad
who's lying on the sofa, shouts.

That crack across the street.
Its perfect straightness packed
tight with moss. I lie back
against the low wall, fit
his house between my feet.

Divorce 1945

1.
As I open the door the first thing
is the sun on the side of the desk,
last polished the day you got back
from the south of England.
Mother had insisted, using a rag
and cream from a tin. Then
your face, and from your shoulder
the metal glint of a wing.
Behind the door in my peep-toe shoes
I try to hear you breathe. Sometimes
I believe you are the quietest man
I've ever known.

2.
Put me in a picture I said.
Just me somewhere on my own
where I can't disappear.
On a beach, my hair blowing hard
against a clear sky. And take me staring
straight at the camera.
A smile doesn't matter.
Just get me all in.

Inside mother's wardrobe

On the highest shelf
there's the white word *Enema*,
next to the naked tribe with wooden lips
inside The New World Encyclopaedia.
A girdle in a cardboard tube, flesh-tinted
Playtex. Yardley. Diamante.
Fenwick's Haberdashery.
Nameless things further in
wrapped in tissue
wrapped in plastic.
Right at the back

red crocodile
one cool fur sleeve
and a man who is not my father.

Marksmen

I'd been snogging the dodgem-greaser
behind the waltzer all night. When I got back

it had happened in Texas - bang in the middle
of Take Your Pick. I'd missed it; was livid.

Three purple hickeys coming up on my neck.

Brenda

Brenda had
aplomb. She in turn
had a crush on Mavis
who was doing five A Levels
at once. Brenda
never did backcomb.
I dream of her

  to the point of

  until we

Just last night
she cried out to me
"I m exhausted being dreamt.
It's been years".

Aftermath

opening the door   abandoned toys
little piles of stones on the stair
draining dishes   shoes
through the window   in the new grass
the blanket   in shadow now
still holds the warm
shapes of movement   after all this time
you 'd think it would be quiet here

Abstract Painting
(after a painting by Annette Chevalier)

After the storm
we got fat on blue cheese
and lived on
in a muddle of debris
on Coney Island.
The clutter was terrible
but we were determined.
 "I'd rather be here
than stuck on the wall
in some gallery
in the north of England"
my father said.

Beached

Two fish lie close on the shingle.
Yellowing, motionless. No-one knows why,

not even the old who still wear greased wool
or father, squinting, mending the nets.

'The lobster pots are empty' he says;
there's talk of hauling the boat upstairs.

In here the cave breathes like a lung
while I go on waiting for the tide to turn.

Losing It

At the finish we leave her laid out.
Sort of changing into brass Gaz says
and we're in the car park lighting up,
still a bit dazed, like, when this magpie
appears out of nowhere and Gaz swears to God
it's eyeing her jewellery up, which he's got
sealed inside a plastic bag
and I'm going *Howay Gaz, Howay*
with an arm round his shoulder like,
but he just keeps on saying
he wants to go back and rub her,
make a rubbing or something.

The Stone Pickers
(after a painting by George Clausen, 1887)

It's a fiddle job.
Me and Martha
we work it together,
sharing the twilight shift.
Slave labour
for two quid an hour
but it puts the dinner

on the table and
it's cash in hand
at the end of the day,
no questions asked.

He says
Rustic Naturalism's the thing,
so he's Depicting me
in brown and light green,
using Heavy Brush Strokes
for the hem of me dress
in order to giv'is
Solidity. This
has been going on
for the last three weeks
and today something in me
just snapped. Solidity George?
You want to give me
Solidity? Don't you think
these bloody stones in me pinny
giv'is that?

Come close

Look at me lying here.
I can only lie. See how I am

reclining
sideways

like an idle Chinese Mandarin
who has grown one long yellow fingernail

and is beckoning with a smile. Fall
for me. Believe I am edible, ripe.

Come close.
Swallow this.

You

It's the way you look. You look
and make me take four beats
to a breath. Step on a line. Step
on a crack.

Last night I traced the edge
of a pattern on the sheet
without moving, while you still stirred
downstairs. And I recognised Florida
and a dog's head where
the plaster has fallen.
It's all because of the way
you look.

I have a thumbnail
that fits beneath three other nails
perfectly, while at the same time
there's a rhyme that I work
against my teeth with my silent tongue
all day. Because of the way you look
I am making an atlas
of the world in my room.

Apart

This morning I dream his face
is on a sheet of postage stamps
sticking inside my eyelids as I wake.
I lick my lips, slip my arms
into his wedding jacket;
the torn lining is covered
with our life in pictures.

I'm going to speak with his lisp
all day; then whisper the syllables,
separate the vowels of our names.

D.I.Y.

I've spent all week wiring it up
and he hasn't even noticed - too busy
installing an ornamental well
beside the gnomes on the patio,
fitting dimmer-switches
inside the kitchen alcoves.

Two days from now
this house will implode
and when the dust finally settles
I'll be gone on the Metro
with the detonator, the vibrator
and one change of clothes.

My first winter like this

I'm not possessed of charm
anymore. He has removed it,
magicked it so I am charmless.
Witness my lack of lustre, my
dull brooch, my bookishness.
In the long folds
of my everyday coat
my penniless hands stained
with verdigris. Ringless.

Caravan

Once there was an abandoned house.
When is she coming home?
Will she be alright on her own?

I like the distant wall
that crawls over the hilltop
into the sky. Also,
I'm writing sideways up.

3 a.m. was freezing -
the World Service was visiting Stratford -
but I woke again in the condensation
of the caravan that worried them
and violent strangers never crossed my path,
although
a man with a glass eye did knock.

What you want

What you want is a sensible pair
something flat for the summer.
You don't want sling backs.
What you want to do is have that cut,
you don't want it hanging over your face
like that. You don't want to go there.
You don't want to encourage them.
You want a coat on.
You don't want to go round
drawing attention to yourself.
You don't want to be too clever,
too thin. You don't want to be bottom,
last. You want to pack that in,
wash that off, watch it.
What you want is an early night.

You want to wear a bra. You want to be careful.
You want to watch your p's and q's
and you want to think yourself lucky.
You want to keep away from the likes of him.
You want to keep away from the likes of her.
You want to be grateful.
You want to make your mind up
what you want. You want
to start doing your bit round here.

You want to take a hard look at yourself.
You want to listen to what I'm saying.
That's what you want.